First Facts®

Revised
and
Updated

The Solar System

Pluto: A Dwarf Planet

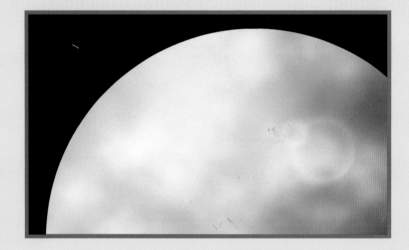

by Ralph Winrich
updated by Thomas K. Adamson

Consultant:
James Gerard
Aerospace Education Specialist, NASA
Kennedy Space Center, Florida

Capstone
press®

Mankato, Minnesota

First Facts is published by Capstone Press,
151 Good Counsel Drive, P.O. Box 669, Mankato, Minnesota 56002.
www.capstonepress.com

Library of Congress Cataloging-in-Publication Data
Winrich, Ralph.
    Pluto: a dwarf planet / by Ralph Winrich.—Rev. and updated/by Thomas K. Adamson.
    p. cm.—(First facts. The solar system)
    Includes bibliographical references and index.
    ISBN-13: 978-1-4296-0727-8 (hardcover)
    ISBN-10: 1-4296-0727-0 (hardcover)
    1. Pluto (Dwarf planet)—Juvenile literature. I. Adamson, Thomas K., 1970– II. Title.
III. Series.
QB701.W46 2008
523.48'2—dc22   2006037427

Summary: Discusses Pluto and its place in the solar system as a dwarf planet.

Editorial Credits
Gillia Olson, editor; Juliette Peters, designer and illustrator; Jo Miller, photo researcher;
    Scott Thoms, photo editor

Photo Credits
The Johns Hopkins University Applied Physics Laboratory & Southwest Research Institute, 17
NASA, 9; Dr. R. Albrecht, ESA/ESO Space Telescope European Coordinating Facility, 5
NASA & ESA/Alan Stern (Southwest Research Institute), Marc Buie (Lowell Observatory), 16
Photodisc, planet images within illustrations and chart, 6–7, 19, 21
Photo Researchers Inc./Science Photo Library/Detlev Van Ravenswaay, cover, 14–15, 20

1 2 3 4 5 6 12 11 10 09 08 07

Table of Contents

Dwarf Planet

Pluto is a **dwarf planet**. A dwarf planet is like a planet but much smaller. Unlike a planet, a dwarf planet is one of many similar objects in its **orbit**. Pluto is very small compared to the eight planets in the solar system. The best pictures show Pluto as a fuzzy ball.

Fast Facts about Pluto
Diameter: 1,440 miles (2,320 kilometers)
Average Distance from Sun: 3.7 billion miles (5.9 billion kilometers)
Average Temperature (surface): minus 382 degrees Fahrenheit (minus 230 degrees Celsius)
Length of Day: 6 Earth days, 9 hours, 17 minutes
Length of Year: 248 Earth years
Known Moons: 3

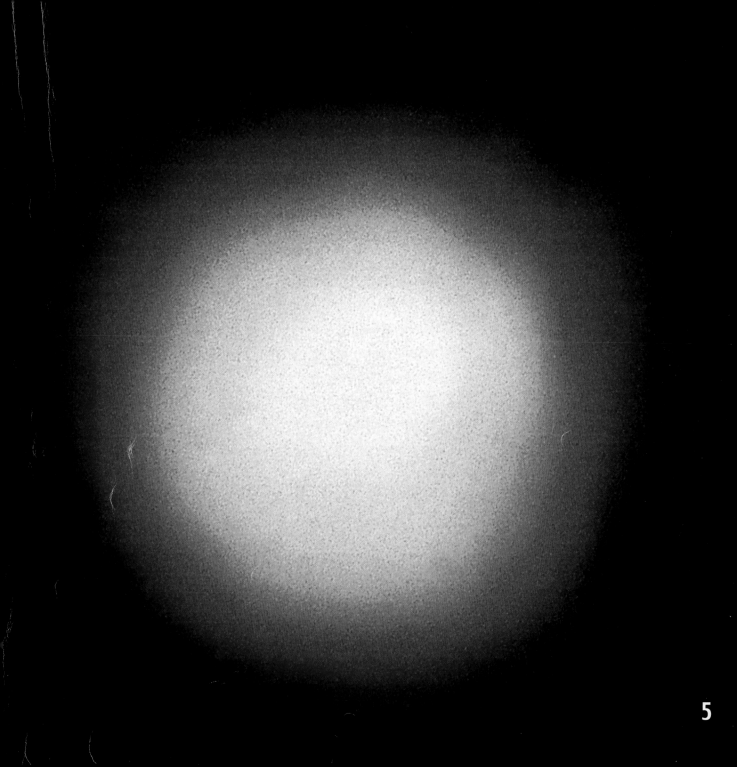

5

The Solar System

The solar system is the Sun and everything that moves around it. Dwarf planets are part of the solar system. Pluto is usually beyond Neptune.

The two other known dwarf planets are Ceres and Eris. Ceres is in the asteroid belt between Mars and Jupiter. Eris is even farther from the Sun than Pluto.

Sun

Mercury

Venus

Earth   Moon

Mars

Jupiter

Saturn

Uranus

Neptune

Pluto
(dwarf planet)

Eris
(dwarf planet)

Asteroid
Belt

Ceres
(dwarf planet)

Pluto's Atmosphere

The gases surrounding planets and dwarf planets are called **atmosphere**. Pluto's distance from the Sun affects its atmosphere. Pluto moves around the Sun in an oval path. When closest to the Sun, Pluto's atmosphere is gas. When far from the Sun, the atmosphere freezes. The frozen gases fall like snow. Pluto then has no atmosphere.

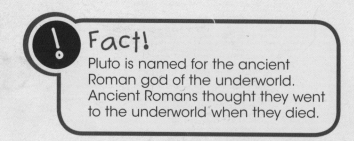

Fact!
Pluto is named for the ancient Roman god of the underworld. Ancient Romans thought they went to the underworld when they died.

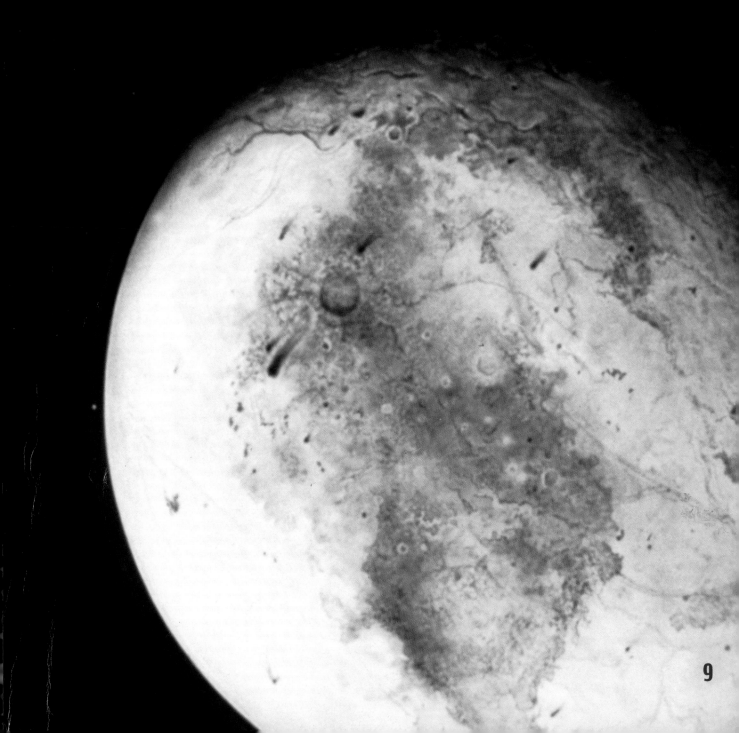

9

Pluto's Makeup

The surface, or **crust**, of Pluto is made of ice. This ice is darker than water ice on Earth. Pluto's ice is made from nitrogen and methane mixed with water. Below Pluto's surface lies a thick **mantle** of water ice. Pluto's **core** is rocky.

Fun Fact!
Pluto is smaller than Earth's moon.

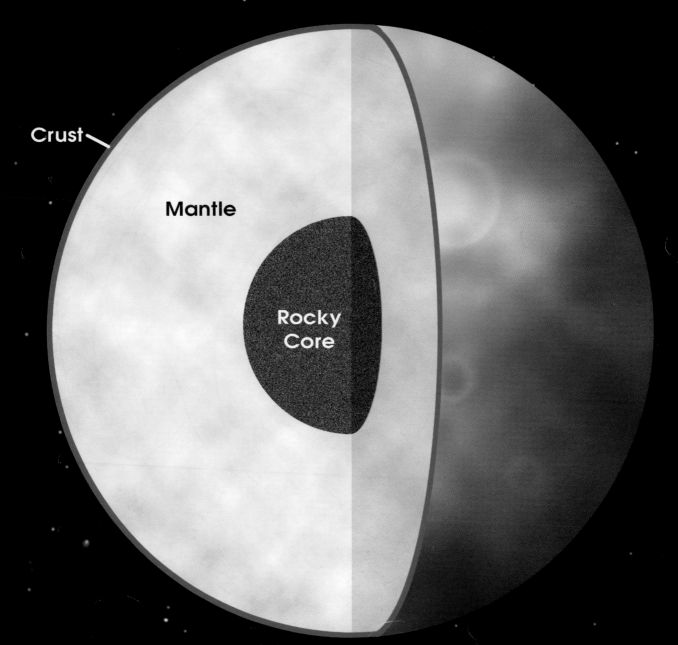

Crust

Mantle

Rocky
Core

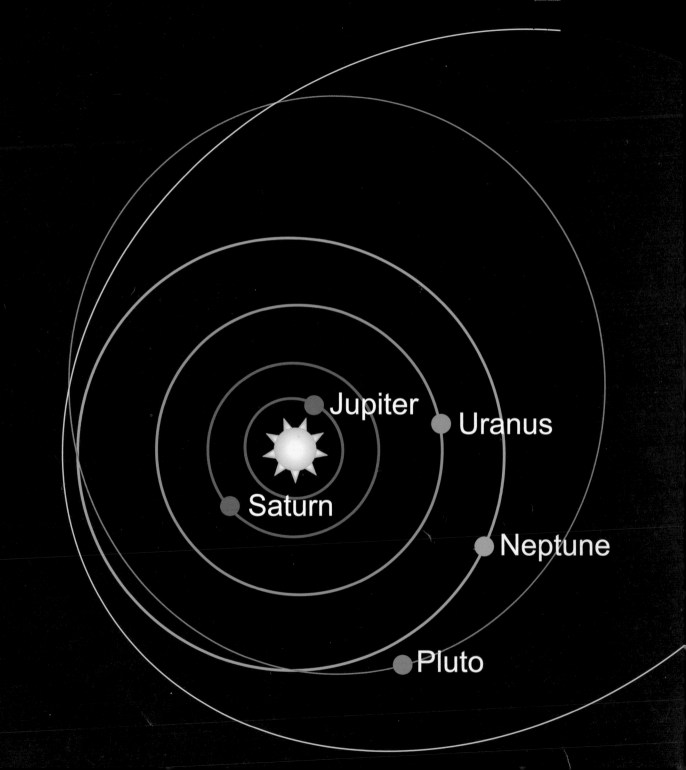

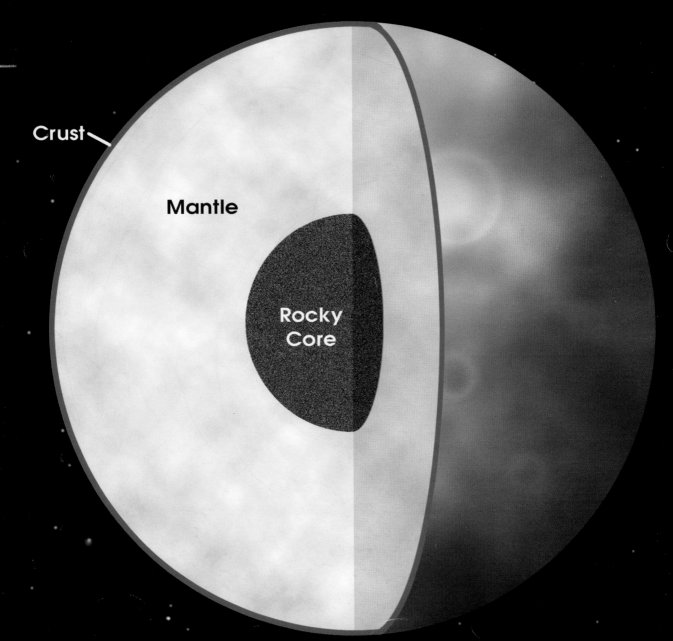

11.

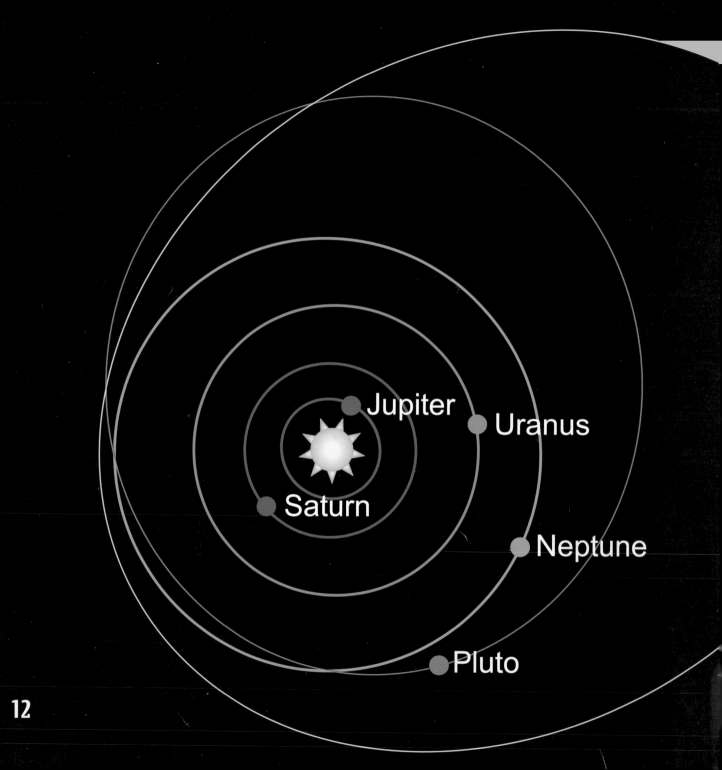

Eris

How Pluto Moves

Pluto takes 248 Earth years to move once around the Sun. Pluto also spins as it travels around the Sun. It takes 6 days, 9 hours, 17 minutes to spin once.

Planets have almost circular orbits. Pluto's orbit is egg-shaped. Eris has an egg-shaped orbit too.

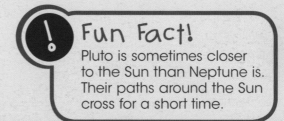

Fun Fact!
Pluto is sometimes closer to the Sun than Neptune is. Their paths around the Sun cross for a short time.

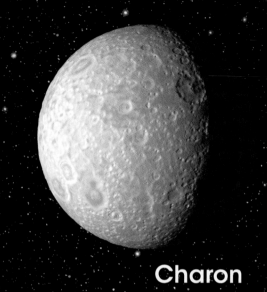

Charon

Pluto

14

Pluto's Moons

Pluto has three known moons. Two of them are very small. Pluto's largest moon is called Charon. Charon is about half the size of Pluto. The same sides of Pluto and Charon always face each other.

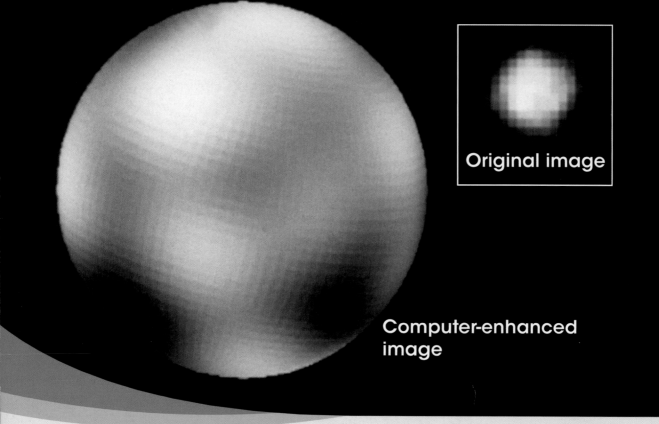

Original image

Computer-enhanced image

Studying Pluto

Even powerful telescopes show little detail of Pluto. They do show bright and dark surface areas. Scientists use computers to make the images clearer.

The **spacecraft** *New Horizons* launched in 2006. It will fly by Pluto in 2015. Scientists are excited to see the first close-up pictures of Pluto.

Comparing Pluto to Earth

Pluto and the other dwarf planets are much smaller than Earth. Ceres is smaller than Pluto. Eris is a little bigger than Pluto.

Scientists want to learn more about this mysterious dwarf planet. And they are likely to discover more dwarf planets in the solar system.

! Fun Fact!
Pluto's diameter is only about half the length of the United States.

Size Comparison

Earth

Ceres

Pluto

Eris

Amazing but True!

Pluto moves around the Sun in a region called the Kuiper belt. Astronomers have discovered more than 1,000 objects in the Kuiper belt. They think there are thousands more. They might even find many more that are larger than Pluto. These objects would likely be called dwarf planets too.

Comparison Chart

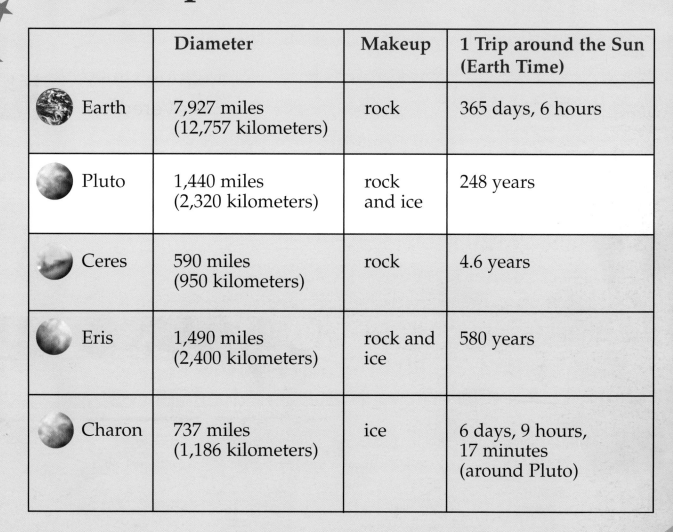

	Diameter	Makeup	1 Trip around the Sun (Earth Time)
Earth	7,927 miles (12,757 kilometers)	rock	365 days, 6 hours
Pluto	1,440 miles (2,320 kilometers)	rock and ice	248 years
Ceres	590 miles (950 kilometers)	rock	4.6 years
Eris	1,490 miles (2,400 kilometers)	rock and ice	580 years
Charon	737 miles (1,186 kilometers)	ice	6 days, 9 hours, 17 minutes (around Pluto)

Glossary

atmosphere (AT-muhss-feehr)—the layer of gases that surrounds some planets, dwarf planets, and moons

core (KOR)—the inner part of a planet or a dwarf planet that is made of metal or rock

crust (KRUHST)—the thin outer layer of a planet or dwarf planet's surface

dwarf planet (DWORF PLAN-it)—a round object that moves around the Sun, but is too small to have cleared its orbit of other objects

mantle (MAN-tuhl)—the part between the crust and the core of a planet or a dwarf planet

orbit (OR-bit)—the path of an object around the Sun

spacecraft (SPAYSS-kraft)—a vehicle that travels in space

Read More

Bryner, Jenna. "Poor Pluto." *Science World*, 9 October 2006, page 5.

Kortenkamp, Steve. *Why Isn't Pluto a Planet?: A Book about Planets.* First Facts: Why in the World? Mankato, Minn.: Capstone Press, 2007.

Orme, Helen, and David Orme. *Let's Explore Pluto and Beyond.* Space Launch! Milwaukee: Gareth Stevens, 2007.

Internet Sites

FactHound offers a safe, fun way to find Internet sites related to this book. All of the sites on FactHound have been researched by our staff.

Here's how:
1. Visit *www.facthound.com*
2. Choose your grade level.
3. Type in this book ID **1429607270** for age-appropriate sites. You may also browse subjects by clicking on letters, or by clicking on pictures and words.
4. Click on the **Fetch It** button.

FactHound will fetch the best sites for you!

Index